FLIGHT

MICHAEL FINKE

Flight

CENTER FOR WRITERS & TRANSLATORS
THE AMERICAN UNIVERSITY OF PARIS

SYLPH EDITIONS

'Airplanes are a dream.'
From *The Wind Rises*, dir. Hayao Miyazaki

IN 1942 ELIAS CANETTI asserted that the 'dream' of flight had 'lost its soul' and been 'realized to death'. *To death* resonates in more ways than one: all who fly tempt the fate of Icarus, while Canetti was writing after the horror of Guernica, the aerial bombing of Shanghai, and the London Blitz. Already in 1927, the year of Lindbergh's solo Atlantic crossing, the narrator of Yury Olesha's short Russian masterpiece, *Envy* (*Зависть*), referred to a nineteenth-century aviation pioneer in lamenting the de-romanticization of flight: 'From earliest childhood the name Lilienthal – transparent and fluttering as the anterior wings of an insect – has had, to my ear, a miraculous sound. This name is linked in my memory with the beginnings of aviation and seems itself capable of flight, as though it were stretched over light bamboo struts. Otto Lilienthal, that soaring man, was killed... A flying machine now looks like a ponderous fish. How quickly aviation turned into an industry!' (Trans. Clarence Brown.)

Olesha's critique of the Soviet production aesthetic followed a Bolshevik campaign linking the promise of progress in post-Revolution (and Civil-War) Russia to technological advances in flight. Long-distance fliers and test pilots were archetypal heroes of the Stalin era that was gaining momentum; the West had its Lindberghs and Earharts. Technological advances have a way of doubling back, however: a decade after NASA's successful moon landing, we were celebrating the human-powered Gossamer Albatross crossing the English Channel (replicating Blériot's feat seventy years earlier). That cross between a dragonfly and a bicycle was oneiric imagery made real; it belongs in a Miyazaki anime.

I am the only one, now, who looks up when a plane passes overhead; my heart sinks when, on a Boeing or Airbus, those privileged with window seats pull down the shades. To fly: some nerve tissue connects that wish with the infant's aspiration to walk upright on two legs, to string together sounds in comprehensible speech, and to be seen doing it; something childishly exhibitionist and self-indulgent that, perhaps, I ought to have outgrown. Now, abruptly, the horizon in view is where I age out of piloting an aircraft; retired from my academic position as scholar and teacher of Russian literature, perhaps it's time to *write* of flight?

In the summer of 1925, the brilliant literary critic and theorist Viktor Shklovsky and the difficult and transgressive fiction-writer Boris Pilnyak, among other prominent Soviet writers, participated in an officially organised project to impress the hinterlands of a still consolidating Bolshevik Russia through contact with airplanes, and then to publicize the experience. These flights were known as *агит-полеты*, or *agit(ational)-flights*. They fit into a broader pattern, whereby Russian and later Stalinist culture exploited the mythologizing power of the still relatively new technology of flight in order to capture the popular imagination and instil a powerful modernizing impulse.

Pilnyak – a pseudonym for Vogau, uncomfortably Germanic when he was breaking into print during World War I – achieved fame with the first significant novel coming out of the Russian Revolution and Civil War, *Naked Year* (*Голый год*). In 1926 he collected his pieces about flying in a volume, *Russia in Flight* (*Россия в полете*); then, in 1927, he published a short novel – in Russian, a *повесть* – titled *Ivan Moscow* (*Иван Москва*) about the areas he had visited on the agit-flights. Pilnyak loved to travel and probably managed more of it than any other contemporary Soviet writer of note, leaving memoirs of voyages to, among other countries and continents, Central Asia, Scandinavia, China, Japan (twice), and the United States. Soon after his arrival in New York, he was hosted at a Metropolitan Club banquet of American literati where, famously, Sinclair Lewis slapped Theodore Dreiser; after a fruitless Hollywood contract that financed purchase of a Ford, he took a road trip back east from California before returning to the Soviet Union with the car and writing a travelogue, *O.K.: An American Novel* (*О- Кей. Американский роман*). 'I am one of those people,' he said, 'who according to Kant fear space and wish to conquer it.'[1] In the year after the agit-flight tour he leapt at an opportunity to fly during his first voyage

to Japan, and in recounting the adventure fabricated something of a heroic self.

Pilnyak's flight from Tokyo to Osaka, courtesy of the Asahi newspaper conglomerate, opens the concluding section of the 1926 travel memoir (or 'novel' as he calls it), *Roots of the Japanese Sun* (*Корни японского солнца*). In that segment, titled 'Japan from an Airplane', Pilnyak declares more than once, echoing Pushkin ('Feast in the Time of Plague' – 'Пир во время чумы': 'There is an ecstasy in battle...'), 'I know the ecstasy of flight', 'the ecstasy of battle with the elements'; 'the higher you go into infinity, the calmer is your blood, there's no sound and there is an inexpressible pleasure of flight'. A nearly catastrophic encounter with a storm gives Pilnyak first-hand experience of the sanguine acceptance of death that he makes a centrepiece of the Japanese national character – the result, he argues, of living with earthquakes and on top of volcanoes. The romantic ethos is more reminiscent of pre-World War I Futurist treatments of flight than of the mid-1920s agit-flights.

In his 1929 story 'Mahogany' ('Красное дерево'), he links the Wright brothers and Lenin in a system of Promethean and Icarus imagery that, if not historically accurate, rings mythopoetically true: 'Once there were some brothers, called Wright; they made up their minds to fly up into the sky, and they perished when they crashed to earth, having fallen out of the sky. They perished, but people have not abandoned their work; they haven't let go of the sky – and people are flying, comrades, they are flying over the earth like eagles! Comrade Lenin perished like the brothers Wright' (trans. Vera T. Reck).

My first flight was in a red, open-cockpit Waco biplane, built just a few years before Canetti's pronouncement. For the short, three-dollar-a-head air-show ride, I was sandwiched between my father and my brother in the front hole of this wood and fabric antique, which a short while earlier had been looping and rolling and trailing smoke in a Snoopy-and-the-Red-Baron gag. Wacos had been built nearby in Troy, Ohio, and now, in 1967, there were still a number of them in the area; in 'hopping rides' they were staging a costume re-enactment of the barnstorming 1920s, when

itinerant individual pilots and small flying circuses would pick
a farmer's field near a town, land their surplus Curtiss Jennies
(more often than not), and offer rides for a few bucks. This was
post-Lilienthal, to be sure, but very much aviation's romantic past.

My next flight was to Albuquerque, on a TWA Boeing 727,
where I was sent to summer with former neighbours whose father
had recently returned from two tours of flying F-100s in Vietnam;
I wore a navy-blue, double-knit sport jacket and tie, and the family
followed me out onto the ramp for snapshots with the Kodak
Instamatic before take-off. When something went amiss with the
connection, perhaps in St. Louis, I was taken by a stewardess –
emphatically a stewardess, not a flight attendant – to a small
private waiting room. Walking down that long corridor with her
stirred me to hide the comic book I was carrying in the jacket's
inner pocket. She left me with a deck of TWA playing cards and a
tin pin: airman's wings.

Pilnyak appeals to me, and he does something with the flight
motif that, as a scholar of Russian literature, I have sought
to understand. Once a sensationally popular and influential
author – for a time he chaired the All-Russian Union of Writers
(Всероссийский союз писателей), and his stylistics were
sufficiently imitated to provoke the coining of a pejorative term,
'Pilnyakovitis' ('пильняковщина'), for the phenomenon – he
hasn't had the posthumous attention paid to other purged Soviet
writers of the 1920s. His ornamental prose tortures syntax at
sentence and higher discursive levels, and it employs peasant
turns of speech and local and interlingual idioms from his travels
or from particular socio-political arenas, as well as outright
neologisms, often frustrating translation by dictionary. His practice
of repetition and self-plagiarism has irritated many readers, but
it has motivations beyond the pragmatic and mercenary (or the
'verbal hooliganism' Maxim Gorky accused him of) and deserves
thoughtful analytic response. One of his most haunting stories, the
violent masterpiece, 'Moist Mother Earth' ('Мать сыра-земля'),
reads as a fascinating metaliterary *study* of repetition in storytelling
and as a function of psychological trauma. As everywhere in

Pilnyak, archaic myth and ritual translates into Revolutionary Russia as intractable symptom, counterbalancing progress.

Russia in Flight captivates as much in depicting a remote Russian interior as in the aerial overcoming of remoteness. In opening, Pilnyak writes that unless you're terrified of flight – believing man was born to crawl, not fly – you don't feel the height, don't notice the speed; the ground below loses all vertical aspect, flattening into two dimensions, transposed into 'a geographical map', that is, encompassed by your vision and cognitively mastered. This, Pilnyak acknowledges, 'has been described by many'.

And yet he does love flying, indeed, he was 'born to fly', and he did it repeatedly – especially as an adolescent – 'in dreams'. The airplane, he says, is the greatest achievement of human genius, because it has translated dreams into reality. Aligning flight with Bolshevik Russia's transformation of human destiny, Pilnyak gives the agit-flight organizers what they paid for: 'the revolutionary dream of 1917 will get to where it has become a reality of the day'; 'our airplane is not at all a Junkers on floats... our airplane is a flying bundle of thoughts and revolution, flying to these places in order to make the revolution, in order to make the revolution with steel and knowledge'. Pilnyak and his comrades cross uncharted expanses where inhabitants ask who the current tsar is. His reportage exploits every possible linguistic sign of backwardness, too, relishing local verbal peculiarities. In the primeval areas to which they have taken the plane, the agit-flight crew overnights in a henhouse where lice devour them while the pilot spins fantastic tales of aviation progress in the West. To those in far-flung villages, 'cut off from the whole world', the plane brings 'knowledge and freedom and height'. The crew will take aloft hundreds of willing peasants and workers, those 'who want to be born to fly and not crawl'.

Today, Bezos, Branson, and Musk can blast folk with the world's fattest wallets into space, not so as to rekindle dreams of flight, but instead, to gin up post-apocalyptic survivalist fantasies of migration to other worlds after we've wrecked this one. They offer a fantasy of escaping death altogether, of living forever, perhaps achievable for a bankroll outweighing anything purchasable on earth. It's both the apotheosis and collapse of translation as metaphor: the entire earthly semiosphere eradicated, except for what might be shot into space on hard drives and in the selective memories of those crossing to another world to establish, presumably, a monocultural colony. I watched Apollo 11 on our small black and white TV; I ate lots of Space Food Sticks, drank Tang, and still admire Velcro; but I'm less interested in space flight than in the shadow of Amelia Earhart's Lockheed Electra that may have been found three miles beneath the south Pacific.

The faded-yellow, four-seat 1950 Piper Pacer I now own – a descendant of aviation's Model T, the Piper Cub, but with wings shortened to permit cheaper manufacturing, and twice the engine for hauling as many as four cramped adults – took its renowned first owner, long-distance flier Max Conrad, four times across the Northern Atlantic in the flights that initiated his ferrying and record-setting career. His wife had majored in French but never travelled to Europe; under financial stress, Conrad sold their Minneapolis home and sent her and their ten children to Geneva, where, shortly after World War II, it was cheaper to maintain them than in Minnesota. Piper gave him a plane for the well-publicized voyage overseas and later advertised the model with photos of his children seated on its wings' leading edges. Conrad went on to cross the Atlantic in light planes roughly 150 times, and the Pacific, 50. Decades earlier he had been struck in the head by a propeller when leaping (and failing) to rescue a passenger headed into his rotating blade; regaining speech and returning to the sky had involved heroic struggle. On these long, restorative flights, he would compose songs, such as 'Flying (Aviation Waltz)', and market the sheet music to admirers:

> I'm flying in the sky
>   Where the clouds dance in the blue,
> The earth floats slowly by
>   Like a fairy land come true.

Or, 'The Endless Sea':

> I wonder why the stars enchant me so
> And make me dream of lands where I must go.

Awful poetry, probably worse with the musical notes, but think of where it comes from, of composing it with one hand on the yoke, over waves, with nowhere to land if the engine quit, always unsure of the weather ahead...

Now the Pacer, its fabric sheenless, drips oil like the beater Ford Falcon I drove at sixteen, though it lacks the Falcon's rust-holes in the floorboards and cigar-ash burns spotting the front seat. Two years ago, with the rear seats removed and packed with a tent, sleeping bag, a folding bike, my laptop for working on a translation of Pilnyak's *Russia in Flight*, and many spare batteries, the Pacer took me camping in the Ozarks, over the Sandia Mountains and Albuquerque, and on to the Zuni Indian Reservation in westernmost New Mexico: my bid at reaching other worlds.

That was almost a flight not taken. A few winters earlier, during a particularly frigid trip from Illinois east to Pittsburgh, ice had blocked the Lycoming engine's breather tube, pressurizing the crankcase, blowing all my oil out past the prop seal, wrecking the crank and a couple of rods as it seized, and marooning me in north central Ohio after a deadstick landing. A foul, flightless year later I had spent as much as the whole plane was worth on an overhaul; so I've bought that airplane twice. Why? How had my life arrived at this summit of irrationality? Tomorrow I'll drive twenty miles to pull out of a leaky, sliding-door hangar with peeling sheet-metal siding this seventy-five-year-old tube-and-fabric translation-into-waking-life of archaic and deeply rooted dreams, as though my soul were still to be found in flight and the machines that permit it.

As when dreaming, I fly alone now: for years my family and friends have deflected offers to go aloft in the Pacer – they don't have the time, they say.

Pilnyak's airplane proves less a conveyance leaping across great expanses of Russian territory than a time machine, capable, even as its visit jolts villagers into the future, of taking him into the past. Traversing geographic distance becomes a trip back in time.

Pilnyak sees factories that date back to Ivan the Terrible, the Stroganovs, and Peter the Great. The proletariat here is a 'half-proletariat', pouring out iron by hand. Entire villages are infected by syphilis. In Usolye, hunters dig up corpses of children, bite off a hand, dry it, and carry it as a talisman against 'the hand of the law, and the paw of the bear'. The town is plagued by arsonists, opponents presumably to the new political order; serfdom has disappeared only ten years before. Here all eras are curiously jumbled together: 'We're not rich in dates, with us everything is at best yardsticked by decades' – an exemplary metaphor conflating space and time. The agit-plane introduces natives to the language of flight, and the progressive worldview encoded in that language, but Pilnyak also brings back to his readers unfamiliar idioms of a world thought extinct.

The airplane-as-time-machine turns 'hours into minutes': according to Pilnyak, it goes so fast that the rotation of the earth must be taken into account as component of its speed (they are actually flying at around 100 mph). The crew keeps its watch set to Moscow time; although they've been travelling East, and so Moscow time lags Komi by a couple of hours, in the narrative's symbolics keeping to Moscow time ensures they remain culturally ahead of these people and places (today Komi keeps Moscow time). Time, more than space, sets Pilnyak apart from the remote provincials he is visiting by air. Pilnyak remembers his childhood, when the temperance society brought the first gramophone to his ancient town south of Moscow, Mozhaisk; his father had feared that little Boris would suffer psychic damage if he saw that amazing machine – but he relented and allowed it. Now Pilnyak sees his child-self in the 'freebooters' gathered on the bank to observe his Junkers, and he knows that in another twenty-five or thirty years they will write of the airplane just like he writes of the gramophone.

In the mid-1970s I was getting through college on my own, aided by generous scholarship funding, modest loans, a work-study library job, and a side gig bussing tables and dishwashing at a Ramada Inn. I still possess the five-by-seven yellow notepad listing every expenditure, down to the occasional dime for a game of pinball, that I kept in my first year, during which, severely near-

sighted, I muddled through a month or so of classes with only one lens in my wire-rimmed eyeglasses, having shattered the other and being reluctant to pay for a replacement. I tried to get by without purchasing all required course books, too: a failing proposition.

An hour of flight would cost the same as that thick lens. To reach the airport meant cycling up a very big hill overlooking the Finger Lake and town below it, and then a gentler climb to the sleepy but towered field; five miles of punishment to arrive at the rental and training operation. I had the ten dollars for a 'discovery flight', and so it happened right then. The gruff, short, rotund owner of the operation took the co-pilot's seat of a brand new Piper Cherokee Warrior, a low-winged, wonderfully docile four-seater – as it would turn out, by far the newest plane I would ever fly.

'Now, how do control surfaces move and what will happen if you pull back on the yoke? Which way does the throttle go to increase power?'

After I moved my hands, responding in pantomime, he beamed: 'You see, you already know it all!'

In flight I followed him ever so lightly on the controls, and he had me perform a few turns, climbs, and descents. After fifteen minutes he proclaimed, 'You're a natural!'

I knew better, but what if it was true?

A newly hired young instructor named Art was seated in the back to learn salesmanship, and it was to him I was handed off. In thirteen lessons – kept short, no doubt in sensitivity to my budget – I progressed to passably consistent landings and was nearing a first solo flight. This meant adapting to winds aloft by crabbing to trace nicely rectangular traffic patterns at the correct altitude; coordinating rudder and aileron in turns and hitting targeted airspeeds; levelling off and flaring at the right height above touchdown; adding a carefully timed dose of rudder at the last moment (as the fledgling instructor taught it) to take the crosswind correction out and track in line with the runway; and avoiding big bounces, or failing that, managing them without porpoising, going around as needed. Emergency procedures had to be practised. The upstate New York landscape always thrilled, especially late in the day, when the low angle of the sun brought out the hills' contours, and clouds and their shadows moved by quickly, with the slanting showers trailing below some of them sprouting rainbows. I always knew where I was, or could figure it out quickly, oriented by the north-south lying Finger Lakes, each distinctively shaped and usually a frigid slate in colour, but varying into warmer hues with the right sky conditions. Coasting downhill back home afterwards was also exhilarating.

 A good flight that did not happen: a drizzly day, with the sky occasionally opening to show blue beyond the thin overcast; I did not know whether it would be flyable, but shy of phoning, I mounted my ten-speed and pedalled to the field.

 'Why didn't you call?' Art asked when I came through the door, dripping. And then he sat me at a table, poured two cups of coffee, and proceeded to deliver a ground-school lesson on VFR weather minimums (flight by visual reference), and how to access current conditions and forecasts: the words for all those atmospherics, and what they meant for when I'd be deciding to go – or not go – on my own.

 After a few more lessons, as I approached the *solo* threshold, my self-doubts ballooned. I pled poverty and quit. What stopped me was a customary fear: less of flying than of failing. I wasn't afraid of the sky, or plummeting to earth from it; I'd imagine the shame, not the pain of a crash, a version of the insecurity that gave me halting, reticent speech in the languages – Russian, principally – that I was studying. At night, I'd dream of flight to spectacular heights, consummated with velvety landings, and just as frequently I'd string together loquacious German or Russian.

The airplane's conquering of horizontal space is obvious, Pilnyak says, but we need also to consider how it conquers the vertical space of intellectual and cultural development. Its nose, seen head on, looks like a human skull: a symbol, he reminds us, of wisdom. In the Bolshevik cultural imaginary, this motif of the wise skull associates the airplane with the recently deceased Lenin, whose prominent forehead, bald, distinctive cranium, and wisdom were front of mind. The airplane's altimeter shows not elevation above the earth, but the cultural gap to be bridged between Tolstoy and Lenin, on the one hand, and the illiterate Mordvins, on the other; that is, by metonymy, the distance between *readers* of Tolstoy and Lenin – and by implication, Pilnyak's own readers – and the backward locals visited by the agit-flight. What the Junkers

carries from village to village is the 'blessing of culture'. After a 200-mile flight over land in a seaplane (supposedly a record at the time), now among speakers of the Finno-Ugric Zyrian language of Komi – a toponym Pilnyak puns into the interlingual 'Komi-mort', or 'land of the dead' – Pilnyak has had enough of flying and decides to return to Moscow by steamer and rail. He urges the progressive youth he finds here to go study 'not for their own sakes, but for the sake of our Russian culture'. And they do go: he departs in the company of 150 students heading to university. He has accomplished an aerial voyage to the underworld, and his return with them by surface transport from the previous century is no failure: in mythic terms, they are rescued.

Pilnyak recycles much of this material in *Ivan Moscow*, but that narrative abounds with Oedipal motifs and atavistic returns that more than counterbalance themes of progress through revolution, flight, scientific advance, and education. He repeats verbatim many passages from *Russia in Flight*: there are the same mammoth bones, the hands bitten from children's corpses, the Stroganov factories; time has been frozen, salted in the mines. But the rock in those mines also contains radium, which promises a spectacular future of limitless atomic energy and displaces the airplane as a marker of progress. Ivan Moscow directs the mining, refinement, and study of the radium. A native of Komi, 'Moscow' is his family name, but also his back story: he went to the city Moscow to study, helped make the Revolution, and fought in the Civil War. During that conflict, in a typhus delirium he had a passionate tryst with a girl whom he will unknowingly meet again and fall in love with a decade later, when he is back in his native region, directing the mine and laboratory. But now his body is succumbing to syphilis, inherited from his father and endemic in the region, and he arranges transport by air and rail to Moscow for a medical consultation: he wishes to learn if he can marry. If syphilis and his last name derive from his biological father, his 'real mother' he considers the city of Moscow, where he entered history in fighting for the Revolution; this figures Lenin (and Commissar of Education Anatoly Lunacharsky) as symbolic fathers. The family plot is doubled by the fliers: the pilot with whom he returns to Moscow will visit his pilot father, for whom he has been substituting, because the father has been grounded, diagnosed by doctors as having 'flown himself out', or flown beyond his physical and emotional limits –

a pseudo-aero-medical condition, presumably of Pilnyak's imagination, and perhaps modelled on the concept of writing oneself out.

Meanwhile, the city of Moscow, rather than appearing the antithesis of Komi, has fallen into grim decadence: it's a place of dystopian back alleys, suicides, drugs, prostitution, black masses, and muggings. Ivan is attacked at one point by a robber gang that, repeating the story's motif of returns and non-recognitions, includes one of his comrades-in-arms from the Civil War. Moscow utterly bewilders him and becomes the site of his collapse, which culminates bizarrely in his loving embrace of a three-thousand-year-old mummy that has been circulating there and which he misapprehends for his beloved, who was herself a return from the past. The mummy had been brought back from Egypt by a professor of history, who disposed of it when he noticed that it was phosphorescent and emanating a smell; it has since passed from hand to hand, until Ivan encounters it at the lodging of the pilots. On the flight back to Komi, the airplane explodes over its destination in a thunderstorm, killing both Ivan and pilot.

Ivan's final 'collapse of energy' echoes the story's opening citation of an explication of a law of energy by Frederick Soddy, the Nobel-winning chemist and social thinker who worked on radioactivity and isotopes. The back story of the mummy's appearance in Moscow and circulation follows the Soddy quotation, suggesting that the mummy's ceaseless, odorous, and phosphorescent decomposition twins radioactivity. Rotting human flesh, which Ivan Moscow also suffers as a result of his inherited syphilis, becomes thematically intertwined with the story's radium motif and its promise of hitherto undreamt-of progress. At some level, Pilnyak's father was right about that gramophone: both flight and atomic energy incite dangerous regressions in tandem with technological advance.

And I'm a child, sitting across from my father as he glues together the plastic parts of a Sopwith Camel. I reach for a wing, and he diverts me with a scrap of paper and a pencil.

'Here's how you can draw a biplane, it's real easy.'

His flying had ceased when I was born.

Among my oldest memories: a bedroom ceiling from which were suspended some twenty-five plastic models, many assembled at that table by my father while I watched and learned about the distinctive odour, if not the intoxication, of glue-sniffing; giving them away to friends on the street when the family furniture store went bankrupt and we moved from Fairborn, a town bordering Wright-Patterson Air Force Base (for some reason my mother declared that the models could not accompany us); watching the annual air show at Wright-Pat from the rooftop of our one-storey hilltop home; the fantasy that my father, a desk-jockey Air Force reservist who had learned to fly privately, would be called up and asked to fly a fighter jet specially equipped with a child's seat in the back.

'Could you ever be assigned to fly a fighter jet?'
'No.'
'If there were a big war and they ran out of pilots, what then?'
'Well, maybe ... '

And among my oldest dreams: taking flight with arms as wings from the jungle gym in the back yard, from which I had once fallen and knocked myself out; watching as one of the massive B-52s based at Wright-Pat crashed into our house – this latter dream perhaps retroactively shaped by a miraculously nonfatal B-52 crash on approach to landing that occurred after we moved away, or by the more serious incident, fifteen years earlier, in which an F-104 Starfighter whose pilot had ejected plummeted into a house in nearby Beavercreek, killing two children, one about my age. With flight, as with swimming in a warm, gently undulating sea, or sailing on a long run, you sometimes get that feeling that this is a dream while you're doing it; and then later, seated at your desk, you again experience the sensation of floating, the rocking and the fluidity – flight translating dream back into reality.

My father's boyhood scrapbooks of World War II aircraft lie boxed in my basement, as do three decades of *Flying*, from the late 1940s forward; having leafed through every issue, I can claim to have been reading the magazine since before I was born. Though I have said that his flying ended with my birth, the real cause was the sharp decline of his own father's business, a low-end furniture store catering to the airmen and civilian employees at Wright-Pat: Dad's maroon Stinson Voyager, an airplane of the same vintage and similar in design to the one I would buy fifty years later, had to be sold. (When they finally went bankrupt seven years later, my grandparents lost their house. Our lawnmower happened to be located at the store when the sheriff locked it up, and so was auctioned off – about which my mother griped for decades.)

Yet every rare once in a while Dad would sneak in a short lesson at a nearby strip. I know this because he took me along once, and I sat – contrary to Federal Aviation Regulations – on a vinyl cushion in the windowless baggage compartment of the two-place Piper Colt trainer while he practised take-offs and landings. All I could see was his hand reaching up to spin the trim handle above his head – a mysterious device. The flight cost ten dollars, and I was not to tell my mother. I figured it was the expenditure that worried him – they had just scissored a bunch of credit cards and sworn to resist superfluous spending – but it may have been the fact of having taken me up without her permission. My childhood involved many Sundays spent parked by a local airport, listening to the tower frequency, learning to identify makes and models, collectively fantasizing about the day when Dad would buy a Cherokee 6, big enough to transport the whole family; Saturdays were spent trailing Mom as she wasted a realtor's time viewing houses for sale but far out of our reach – preferably with swimming pools.

In Russia as in the West, early-twentieth-century Modernist artists, writers, and critics were drawn to airplanes and flight. Franz Kafka and Gabriele d'Annunzio attended the 1909 Brescia Air Show, and in 1910 a young Viktor Shklovsky was among spectators at the first Aviation Week in St. Petersburg. The flashy Shklovsky went on to write experimental fiction and co-found what became the Russian Formalist movement in literary theory and criticism; he may be best known in the West for his analysis of the playful narrative devices of Laurence Sterne's *Tristram Shandy* and his theory of art as 'making it strange' (остранение). Reading him is like watching aerobatics: impossible twists and turns, and empowering generalizations and analytic tools that enable the budding critic to take apart a narrative and say true things about its workings without much knowledge of author or context.

By the time that Shklovsky, like Pilnyak, was commissioned to participate in the agit-flight project, flying machines held little appeal for him, and this remained true half a century later: early in his memoir *Once upon a Time* (Жили-были) he writes of seeing an image of Lilienthal in a turn-of-the-century journal: 'He wanted to fly and broke his legs. One shouldn't fly'. Unhappy injunction!

Shklovsky placed a few agit-flight sketches in the 1926 *Third Factory* (Третья фабрика), and he collected other accounts in the section 'Road Races and Flights' ('Пробеги и пролеты') in *Hamburg Reckoning* (Гамбургский счет – perhaps better rendered: *An Honest Accounting*). He was dispatched by the magazine *Ogonyok* (Огонек) to Kharkov (Russian for Kharkiv) to catch up by air with the caravan of a cross-country auto rally: 'I wanted to sleep, not wax enthusiastic', he complains of his 7 a.m. aerodrome appointment. His depiction of the aircraft is deliberately unhelpful: the Dornier they are flying has wings supported by wires, whereas the Junkers that has just taken off for Koenigsberg does not, while the Dornier has wicker seats for eight passengers – and that's the sum of it, an illogical comparison of wing structure with cabin seating. No verbal portrait, no fetishizing the machine, no wonder at flight; still less such fundamental information related to the story as *why*. Instead, Shklovsky sleeps three of the four hours aloft – no dreams reported – and to make up for his truculence cites an anecdote from Hans Christian Andersen, who wonders at the travelling speed of the then new conveyance of the train, which passes through an entire duchy while Andersen is taking one pinch of snuff. 'Since the 100th anniversary of the railroad occurred recently, take this anecdote... in place of a description of the flight to Kharkov'. Flight merely repeats an experience well documented one century previously. He repeats this in opening the next piece, 'Aboard the Airplane' ('На самолете'): 'Describing flight is hard, since it's already been described many times over'.

Further, the view from above proves misleading: 'From an airplane what's visible is not what's important, but that which there's a lot of.' This contradicts the agit-flight mission, which is expressed in Pilnyak's map metaphor, and also by subsequent scholarly understanding of the function of aerial perspective in

Soviet cinematography of the 1930s, according to which the aerial view translates into a graspable whole a geographic, political, and cultural entity whose vastness tends rather to incoherence, and 'expresses control over the landscape, rendering it tame', thereby helping to establish a unified state in the cultural imaginary.[2] An emphasis on the airplane's potential for conquering vast space was there in the earliest, most influential post-revolutionary discussions of flight; it was a notion that circulated worldwide and translated well. Flights that crossed the country, spanned oceans, or circled the world – no matter how long they took – were especially celebrated. In the United States, when the first transcontinental air service was launched by TAT in the late 1920s, the Secretary of Commerce pressed a button in Washington D.C., transmitting an electronic signal that the Ford Trimotor ('Tin Goose') should be launched: all was connected and under central control. In early Soviet Russia, Leon Trotsky was one of aviation's most important boosters: as early as the winter of 1922-23, he had urged the building of civilian and military air fleets, incited a press campaign to gain public support, and organized a civic institution to help finance it, the Society of Friends of the Air Fleet (Общество друзей воздушного флота, or ОДВФ).[3]

But despite all this, what Shklovsky sees from above, at least at first, is a peculiar incoherence: a 'jumble of broken crockery', a 'pile of lumber seen from one end'. In *Third Factory* he writes: 'The clouds and the land are unattractive. There's nothing aesthetic in this perspective'.

A fair-weather flier, I love the view from above: the everchanging intersection of earth and sky, grasping how landmarks are arrayed in relation to one another, a fading concept in today's era of track-up displays on a cell phone – who still reads the paper map of Pilnyak's analogy? The coherence of exterior space translates inwards: that broader picture puts me back together as well.

Shklovsky's locals enjoy no intellectual gains from going aloft. In 'The Village Longs for the City' ('Деревня скучает по городу') they flock to landing aircraft 'as if money was being given out'.

Rather than a vector toward progress, the airplane manifests a retrograde craving for anything from the city. This extends even to language: everything new is relished, and especially foreign words, so that while Shklovsky and his company call their vehicle a 'самолет', a word of Russian origin literally meaning 'self-flier', the peasants insist on using the Western 'аэроплан' ('aeroplane'). Meanwhile, older villagers conceive the airplane as a 'spy on heaven', so that their potentially positive curiosity devolves into a backward cosmology rooted in religion.

Only the last two sketches of 'Road Races and Flights' grudgingly execute their propagandistic mission. 'Aboard the Airplane' finally provides a coherent description of the aircraft: the size of its engine, the fact that it has dual controls, a passenger cabin, and a visage like a 'dull-nosed fish'. In Shandean fashion, it is only at the very end of the cycle that Shklovsky finally relates his plane's name, 'Facing the Village' ('Лицом к деревне'); only now does he reveal what might rightly have been the point of departure for the series, explaining that he has been aboard an agit-plane. Although flying proves a most unpleasant mode of transportation – Shklovsky likes only the take-off; descent is unpleasant; turbulence extremely so; and turning makes him want to grab hold of his neighbour – the airplane is, after all, proclaimed a useful cognitive tool. The view from above has a *defamiliarizing* function: 'everything...seems completely new'. He predicts: 'In Italian painting, beside normal perspective, there was also "horseman's perspective" and "frog perspective". In the future of painting there will be the perspective of a flier.'

Touting the aesthetic impact of a new, aerial viewpoint on the rutted mind is utterly consistent with Shklovsky's theory of the purpose of art as *остранение*, variously translated as *making it strange*, *defamiliarization*, or *estrangement*. But this still diverges from what the commissars sponsoring the flights intended. Only at the very end does he supply a few lines of the requisite language. Flight facilitates 'the joining of city with country – the only salvation of culture'; it allows travel to places that otherwise would have to be reached by a pair of oxen; from above one can view and diagnose the ill earth, 'sick with ravines, like syphilis', which can lead to water projects bringing (agri)culture to the steppe. In closing, he identifies himself and the flight crew with

the hated machine: 'The peasants question us...', he writes; '"Us" – that's the agit-plane "Facing the Village".'

Shortly after I took my first academic position, on days without classes I started sneaking twenty miles west on the highway bisecting the city to the Spirit of St. Louis airport; not, however, without enjoining my instructor *never* to tell *anyone* that he was teaching a young university faculty member – nobody must know of these hours diverted from research and course preparation. When I did come out, so to speak, to my colleagues, I composed a ready answer for their 'Why?': I fly because it's safer than sex – *pause* – and cheaper than psychoanalysis. (It was a better line back during the HIV/AIDS terror, and when I myself was immersed in scholarship involving Freud and Lacan.) Notwithstanding the lore regarding oversexed pilots, there has long been an understanding of flight as taking the place of sex, quite a twist in the fear-of-flying metaphor. Wilbur Wright claimed that he didn't 'have time for both a wife and an airplane'.

'You look so happy!' my wife said, wonderingly, when many years later I showed her a photo a friend had taken as I looked back briefly while landing his Citabria at a pretty grass strip in central Illinois.

Pilnyak's *Ivan Moscow* recycles the Komi flight with allusions to Tolstoy's *Anna Karenina* (however odd that may seem), the Bible, and H. G. Wells's *The World Set Free*, a 1914 novel about a world war in which atom bombs are dropped by hand from the open cockpits of biplanes, creating an apocalypse that leads to technological utopia. Pilnyak's story juxtaposes radio-chemistry and the Old Testament, scientific advance and troubling continuities with the past; evolution and grim degeneration go hand in hand, with the result that the very positive image of youth departing to study in the capital that ends *Russia in Flight* is overwhelmed by imagery of decay, mis-cognitions, tragic sacrifice, and regressive returns. The airplane may be a dream realized, but in *Ivan Moscow* that dream is more traumatic nightmare than futuristic fantasy, its realization the surfacing of repetition-compulsion and other atavistic workings of body and unconscious mind.

Did Pilnyak participate in the 1920s Moscow Freudian circles that flourished prior to Stalin's cultural clampdown? Influence shows in 'Moist Mother Earth', and his piece about the writer's craft in the 1930 volume *How We Write* (*Как мы пишем*) suggestively echoes Freud's 1908 'The Relation of the Poet to Day-Dreaming' in ascribing his own creativity to habits or procedures by which he accesses the primary processes of his unconscious. Pilnyak writes first thing in the morning, while still on the boundary between sleep and wakefulness, always regretting that he cannot get it all down, and he takes special measures to remain in contact with the world of sleep and dreams. His regime appears designed to facilitate regression to a child self: abstaining from coffee, tea, and alcohol, he puts himself on an infant's milk diet. 'My very best stories, tales and novels were written, of course, in childhood, because it was then, and with the greatest force, that I felt the creative instincts', he asserts; and though he supposedly read thirty or more hydrotechnical books while working on his 1930 Socialist Realist production novel, *The Volga Falls into the Caspian Sea* (*Волга впадает в Каспийское море*), he says that he 'saw that novel in my dreams'. For Pilnyak, writing fiction, like flight, figures as a dream realized.

Something similar is happening in the oneiric manga films of Hayao Miyazaki, which invariably involve flight, with his last directly featuring airplanes. Miyazaki's father manufactured aircraft parts during World War II, like the boy's father in *The Boy and the Heron*, who makes canopies for the Mitsubishi Zero fighter. In *The Wind Rises*, about the designer of the Zero, that Mitsubishi engineer appears first as a child dreaming of flight, and at key moments he encounters his idol, the Italian aeronautical pioneer Giovanni Caproni, in his dreams. It's not so much that he sees Caproni in his sleep, but rather that he inhabits the same oneiric space as the fatherly Caproni: their visions of flying machines merge. And earlier, there was *Porco Rosso*, reminiscent of such interwar Hollywood aviation classics as *Wings*, *Hell's Angels*, and *Dawn Patrol*.

From *Porco Rosso*'s promotional posters: 'A pig who doesn't fly is just an ordinary pig', and 'If you fly, you can see'. From its dialogue, involving a romantic rivalry between aces: 'You're a dreamer. I like that in a man.'

The day after I arrived in Moscow during the turbulent 1990s, for a summer of research in the former Lenin Library, I was offered a ride in a Sukhoi fighter jet, priced at $10,000. The Sukhoi executive proposing the flight disparaged my jet-lagged Russian to the intermediary who had introduced us, as though I could not hear or understand him. I declined.

Later in my stay I took the metro to its far northwest reaches to visit Tushino Airfield, where I had learned there was still a paramilitary DOSAAF (ДОСААФ) aeroclub, descendant of the organization Trotsky had initiated. The place was quiet, rundown, more a junkyard populated by retired air force equipment than an active airport – it would soon be repurposed altogether – but during most of the Soviet period Tushino hosted an annual celebration of Soviet air power attended by hundreds of thousands. I found the club's office; outside were parked two well-used Yak-52 trainers, and inside sat a club officer, smoking. Yes, he told me, it would be possible to arrange dual instruction in one of the Yaks; the cost would be three U.S. dollars per minute, in cash. I had never seen flight time charged by the minute and figured that this tariff bore no relation to what the club charged natives; and this was six times the hourly rate to fly the old Cessna Skyhawk in which I currently partnered back in St. Louis, about whose maintenance I had confidence. I couldn't bring myself to do it (which I still regret).

At the end of the 1990s I began to contemplate a career move from academia or attempting overlapping careers: the aviation industry was heating up and commuter airlines were snapping up low-hour commercial pilots. At the flight-training and rental operation where I was instructing a few hours a week, I met an obstetrician who was moonlighting for a commuter and two lawyers who flew charters. But then in 2000 the stock market bubble burst, followed by the blow of 9/11: my aviation employer sold his six planes and little helicopter at a loss, defaulted on his loans and rental arrears, declared bankruptcy, and found a government job; friends who had recently landed airline jobs were furloughed. I settled back

into a book project on Anton Chekhov and began looking for scholarly angles on flight. There were classic Soviet films to watch, long-distance and test pilots to read about, as well as the female aces who flew combat missions over Stalingrad, and the Night Witches who shut down the engines of their wood and fabric biplane trainers to glide silently over German bivouacs and drop small bombs; the Futurist opera *Victory over the Sun* (*Победа над солнцем*), Constructivist Vladimir Tatlin's 'Letatlin' ('Летатлин'); and, of course, those extraordinary agit-flights.

'So, I hear you're a flier,' my grandmother greeted me on my last visit to her nursing home.

St. Louis was surrounded by fine general aviation airports, and over the years I bought into a series of partnerships that had me flying out of several. Three of them closed during my two decades there: Arrowhead, St. Charles Municipal, and Weiss. Before 9/11 you could fly over Busch Stadium during a Cardinals baseball game low enough to grasp uniform colours and the players' movements, and also fly circuits around the Arch. Returning from a long flight out west in a Cessna 182, the sun was setting, shadows putting hilly terrain to the north in high relief; flying past the reddened bluffs mirrored in the Mississippi by Grafton and Elsah and on toward Alton Regional, I surprised myself in acknowledging this sight as beautiful as any I had seen over desert and mountains. Circling the city, I might join with bald eagles up north by the Winfield dam. And every Sunday the owner of Creve Coeur Airport rang the bell at noon for an inexpensive barbecue lunch, which he prepared, and all the TWA captains and McDonnell-Douglas engineers based there had their hangar doors open, exhibiting one of the finest collections of antique, classic, and homebuilt airplanes in the United States.

At the peak of my flying life, a few years before moving away, I became partners in a later model of just such an aircraft as my father had dreamt of acquiring. It was a six-seat Cherokee, but better, faster, with retractable gear and the latest avionics.

If I had answered that question 'Why?' less facetiously, I'd have said that it all must go back to him. Three fourths of the pilots, when asked why they fly will, in one way or another, begin their answer: 'Well, my father…'

On one of his last visits we went for a ride, heading up the Mississippi northwest of the city on a clear, smooth day. Once beyond airspace restrictions and at a comfortable altitude I motioned to the yoke on his side of the cockpit and suggested he try a few tentative turns; he soon frowned and said, 'I don't like it.' And so I radioed Spirit tower and we headed back to land. He had flown in the 1950s, and this panel was incomprehensible to him. Ageing had left him rigid, comfortable only when following daily routines that culminated in the neighbourhood bar; there he might happily repeat an old story about flying, but taking the controls again was another matter. By then, too, all the relics of his own brief pilot's career had been destroyed in the aftermath of a nasty second divorce. If not, I'd have his logbook, old charts and flight computer – a kind of slide rule tailored to aeronautical calculations – boxed in the basement, along with his magazines and his ashes.

A year after I moved away from St. Louis, one of the partners in that Cherokee filled it with fathers and sons and flew down to a trout-fishing resort in Arkansas. I had been there several times on daytrips for lunch in its restaurant overlooking the White River and a stroll along the pristine waterway. It had an immaculately groomed, long and wide grass strip, but because of wires at one end and the Ozark hill at the other, landing had to happen in one direction, following a bend in the river rather than flying a conventional traffic pattern – and take-off the opposite way; this usually meant seeing performance degraded by unfavourable winds on either the landing or the take-off, since one normally does both into the wind. When he launched for home, overloaded and no doubt later than planned on a scorching summer day, this former partner crashed into a hillside. Wax, feathers, and proximity to the sun: high temperatures severely diminish a piston engine's power output and cause deadly accidents every year, especially in aircraft overloaded with fathers, teenage sons, and coolers of brown trout.

The Oedipal dimension of flight's unconscious meaning features centrally in Douglas Bond's 1952 *The Love and Fear of Flying*, a post-World War II, psychoanalytically-oriented psychiatric study by a former flight surgeon of 'emotional casualties' and 'flight neuroses' – today's anxiety disorders, panic attacks, and PTSD – among bomber pilots and crewmembers of the Eighth Air Force flying out of Great Britain. In certain cases Bond interprets the airplane as the feminized substitute for an erotic object of incestuous desire; he reads flight as a challenge to and attempted mastery of death, an invitation to dreaded paternal punishment and an 'unbridled' exhibitionistic flaunting of it.

Remember the famous sonnet by the British fighter pilot James Magee, which Ronald Reagan cited at the end of his televised address to the nation when space shuttle Challenger blew up shortly after launch?

> Oh! I have slipped the surly bonds of Earth
>   And danced the skies on laughter-silvered wings;
> [...]
> Where never lark, or even eagle flew –
>   And, while with silent, lifting mind I've trod
>   The high untrespassed sanctity of space,
> Put out my hand and touched the face of God.

One often hears that poem when a flier dies, its citing intended to suggest a profoundly spiritual dimension to flight in a life that, though prematurely ended, achieved something meaningful. In writing of fighter pilots just after the war, Dr. Bond finds, instead, male aggressivity unleashed by mortal combat: 'Every dangerous success is an indulgence of incestuous desires, at the same time as it defies and mocks the authority and power of the father and thereby brings reassurance of omnipotence and of the ability to withstand castration. Pilot Magee's poem shows the exultation he felt when he dared to "touch the face of God" and "got by" with it.' One flies, according to Bond, to be like the father; one flies in defiance of the father and the castrating punishment that is his to mete out; the airplane is a phallic symbol; the airplane stands for the female erotic object. It feels preposterous, but then I remember that the B-29 that delivered 'Little Boy' over Hiroshima, 'Enola Gay,' was named after pilot Paul Tibbets's mother.

If there ever had been a time when my own father loomed as heroic, then that was long lost to infantile amnesia. His aviating stories were few: of failing to 'plant' his Stinson while landing in a crosswind and suffering a groundloop (when a tailwheel airplane pivots around one of the mainwheels, doing a donut and likely dragging a wingtip, or worse, rather than tracking straight down the runway); of nearly putting it into the trees taking off at French Lick, Indiana, after flying down to the resort to pick up his parents on a hot, humid summer day; of getting lost amid thunderstorms in hilly Kentucky. Talking airplanes evoked a fulfilling past, an empty present, and longing: he wanted to, but couldn't, for lack of a more commanding signifier of masculinity. This want only loomed larger over time, as the family teetered on the edge of bankruptcy right up until it broke apart. (Still a student, I was working part-time restaurant and library jobs and mailing checks to help him pay the meagre child support for my youngest sibling and avoid jail.)

In 1996, I took an aerobatics lesson, at a rental and training operation of two McDonnell-Douglas test pilots, one of whom had recently been killed northeast of St. Louis, looping an F/A-18 too low. His partner was pained by this recent loss and working to keep the business venture going for the accident victim's family. A couple of spins and barrel rolls went fine, but the first attempt at a loop provoked intense nausea – and there ended my flying as an extreme sport. A few years later, when a woman with whom I flew down to Memphis for a memorable date thought to liven things up by provoking me to roll or loop our stolid Cessna, I soberly explained what it meant for an aircraft to be certified for aerobatics, and the ease with which I, untrained, could exceed g limits and pull the wings off this one, which was not so certified. (This probably left her unimpressed.)

    Nor do I much challenge the weather. I can fly on instruments but I enjoy the view above all, so flying in the clouds does not appeal; neither does night flight, where the risks pile up, especially behind only one engine. Ten years ago, while performing the few periodic take-offs and landings required to stay night legal, I suffered an electrical failure on a moonless December night, and with the windscreen frosting up – was I panting? – had no way to turn on the runway lights of the rural Illinois grass strip where I then kept the Pacer. Well, once you've taken off, you've got to land. After three or four passes I put it down smoothly, and – oriented by a single lamp atop a hangar – in the centre of the invisible strip. But I haven't embarked after dark since; these days I don't see so well at night anyhow.

The recent flight to New Mexico was a test of sorts. Above all, of my own ageing frame's flexibility and endurance: two full days in the cramped cabin seated on sagging springs left my back stiff and sore, and climbing in and out of the plane at fuel stops became a chore. I had never flown two long days in a row before, and my last lengthy cross-country had been fifteen years ago, in a faster and better-equipped machine. Getting out of the Pittsburgh area, the ceiling was lower than forecast, making it a challenge to miss the powerplant stacks west of town while staying below the cloud bases by a legal margin. Visibility was poor, and my attitude indicator (an artificial horizon), which would keep me upright if I blundered into the clouds, tumbled; but I had a portable backup and flew on. Headwinds were fierce, so I deviated to the south where forecasts showed them lighter and I would exit the weather sooner. By the time I reached western Kentucky and entered southern Missouri, still flying low for less adverse winds, skies had cleared, but it was beastly hot, and every five or ten miles a field was burning, so I flew into a blinding sun in thick haze. I barely made the unlit backcountry Ozark strip before dark.

The next day I was taking this tailwheel airplane, tricky to land in crosswinds, through Oklahoma, Texas, and the width of New Mexico, where it really blows; and though I was lightly loaded, the high elevations and summer temperatures had me worried about take-off performance after fuel stops. But then I passed through a gap between the mountains east of Albuquerque, and a solitary, well-defined storm cell was crossing my path as I approached the southern slopes of massive Mt. Taylor. I skirted it to the left toward a lowering sun unblocked by the drizzle trailing the real rain, where rainbows sprouted to augment the mesas, buttes, canyons, and scrub. I had never seen the high desert so green; yes, they told me, it had been very wet. There was hardly an elegant landing during the whole trip, a few real bouncers, but I got it down safely, without any go-arounds, and without bending metal.

Pulling the plane into its hangar after the return flight home, I thought how I'd tell my father about it.

Writing was always a hazardous activity in Russia. Pilnyak may have been right about Japan and death and what that flight above mountains in a thunderstorm presaged for him. His fate had probably been sealed in 1926, when he published a story, 'Tale of the Unextinguished Moon' ('Повесть непогашенной луны'), which echoed rumours that Stalin was behind the medical execution, during party-ordered surgery, of the immensely popular military commander Mikhail Frunze. Compromised also by having published abroad (like many others in the 1920s) and by his 'Fellow Traveller' status – the term designated writers who, not members of the Party and of questionable class background, at least tolerated the Revolution – Pilnyak suffered vicious criticism for most of the next decade. Periodically, he would recant and attempt compositions that overtly met critical demands, while often subverting expectations in indirect ways as a master of the counter-narrative. For the last few years of his life he would run into acquaintances who were astonished to find him alive and on the street: premature rumours had spread of his inevitable arrest.

Following his second trip to Japan, completed at the behest of Soviet authorities, in autumn of the peak purge year of 1937 he was taken from his dacha (next to that of his friend Boris Pasternak) in the writers colony of Peredelkino. After six months of imprisonment and interrogation and a fifteen minute trial in which he pled guilty to a fictional list of high crimes that included preparing to assassinate Stalin and Nikolai Yezhov (head of the secret police), as well as espionage for Japan, he was allowed a few last words. He claimed to have 'become a different person'. 'I want to work hard, I want to have paper in front of me on which I could write something of use to Soviet People.' And then he received a bullet in the back of the head.[4]

Endnotes

1. Cited from Ben Hellman, 'The Last Trip abroad of a Soviet Russian Globetrotter: Boris Pilnyak's Northern Journey in 1934', *Russian Literature* LXXI (2012) II: 173.

2. Emma Widdis, 'To Explore or Conquer? Mobile Perspectives on the Soviet Cultural Revolution,' in *The Landscape of Stalinism: The Art and Ideology of Soviet Space*, eds. Evgeny Dobrenko and Eric Naiman (Seattle: University of Washington Press, 2003), 235.

3. See Scott W. Palmer, *Dictatorship of the Air: Aviation Culture and the Fate of Modern Russia* (Cambridge: Cambridge University Press, 2006), 85-102.

4. See Vitaly Shentalinsky, *Arrested Voices: Resurrecting the Disappeared Writers of the Soviet Regime*, trans. John Crowfoot (New York: The Free Press, 1993), 139-57.

A small portion of this essay appeared previously in 'Why I Fly,' *The Common Reader: A Journal of the Essay*, Vol. 7, No. 1.

COLOPHON

THE CAHIERS SERIES · NUMBER 40
ISBN: 978-1-909631-46-5

Series Editor: Dan Gunn
Associate Series Editor: Daniel Medin
Design: SYLPH EDITIONS DESIGN
Set in Giovanni Mardersteig's Monotype Dante

Text: ©Michael Finke, 2024
Images: ©Rachael Plummer, 2024

With thanks to the San Francisco Foundation for its generous support.

No part of this publication may be reproduced in any form whatsoever without the prior permission of the authors or the publishers.

Published by Sylph Editions, London
The American University of Paris | 2024

www.sylpheditions.com   www.aup.edu